Herbert Howells

The 'London' Services

Selected and edited with a preface by David Hill

Novello

NOV445000
ISBN No. 0-7119-8462-X

Music setting by Andrew Parker

Cover design by Michael Bell Design
Cover picture: Westminster Abbey the Quire
© Pitkin Unichrome

The composer's photograph: Reg Wilson

This edition © 2000 Novello Publishing Limited
Published in Great Britain by Novello Publishing Limited

Head office: 14/15, Berners Street, London W1T 3LJ, England.

Telephone: +44 (0)20 7434 0066
Fax: +44 (0)20 7287 6329

Sales and hire:
Music Sales Limited
Newmarket Road, Bury St. Edmunds, Suffolk IP33 3YB

www.musicsales.com

e-mail: music@musicsales.co.uk

Herbert Howells was born in Lydney, Gloucestershire on 17 October 1892.

At the age of eighteen, he became a pupil of Herbert Brewer, Organist of Gloucester Cathedral. In 1912 he was awarded a scholarship to the Royal College of Music and studied under Charles Villiers Stanford, Walter Parratt, Charles Wood and Hubert Parry.

Eight years later, after ill-health forced him to relinquish his position as sub-organist of Salisbury Cathedral, Howells returned to the RCM to teach composition, an occupation which was to interest him until the end of his life. Howells also taught at St. Paul's Girls' School, Hammersmith, and, in 1950, was appointed King Edward VII Professor of Music at London University.

Howells never collected or made direct use of folk songs. He did, however, accept their importance as part of a wider musical heritage but preferred to allow church modes and the pentatonic scale to play a more prominent part in the construction of his output. In works such as the *Fantasia for Cello and Orchestra* (1936) and the *Concerto for String Orchestra* (1938), Howells shows his ability to incorporate a smooth melodic line with an almost disturbing harmonic dissonance.

The move away from secular to sacred music which *Hymnus Paradisi*, possibly his masterpiece, marked, continued into the 1940s with a series of compositions setting Mass texts and Canticles, most notably the *Magnificat* and *Nunc Dimittis* from the Anglican Evensong service. Around twenty settings are known of which the settings for King's College, Cambridge (*Collegium Regale*), St. Paul's and Gloucester Cathedrals are considered by some to be among the finest.

Howells' output for the organ has been accepted as core repertoire and shows a mastery in both style and technique in writing for this medium. The *Six Pieces*, dating from 1940 to 1945, are full of rich dissonance with a romantic twist which is neither pretentious nor superfluous. Here, Tudor influences can be seen as in other works – although they are moulded and adapted to Howells' style.

Herbert Howells died in London on 23 February 1983 at the age of 90. During his life he had been awarded a Collard Life Fellowship (Worshipful Company of Musicians), CBE (1953) and in 1972 was made a Companion of Honour.

David Hill FRCO is a Choral Advisor to Novello. Since 1987 he has been

Master of the Music at Winchester Cathedral. He is also Musical Director of The Bach Choir and Director of the Waynflete Singers. He was Organ Scholar at St. John's College, Cambridge, where he was assistant to Dr. George Guest and studied the organ with Gillian Weir and Peter Hurford. He is frequently invited to direct choral workshops and summer schools, particularly in Britain, the USA, Canada and Australia.

He is co-author of *Giving Voice*, a book on choir training and has made many recordings as conductor, organist and chorus master.

Preface by David Hill

The Services of Herbert Howells are exemplary works in the long British tradition of religious choral music. His musical background brought him into contact with notable figures in the nineteenth-century tradition of church music: he studied the organ with Sir Herbert Brewer at Gloucester Cathedral and composition with Sir Charles Stanford at the Royal College of Music. Illness in his early 20s interrupted the start of his career as a cathedral organist and his focus did not return to concentrate on church music until the early 1940s: only two of the Services were composed before 1941. The Romantic elements of his training blended with the twentieth-century influences of Debussy and Ravel along with the inflections of blues, so creating a unique style that was bound together by a naturally polyphonic voice. Long melismatic phrases give the works a distinctive elegance, while the harmonic palette is always finely chosen to provide a sense of the English language but with a French accent.

Howells wrote the Services for particular choirs and particular buildings. Any interpretation of the Services for choirs today must consider the individual nature of the acoustic in which they are performed. Whatever the character of the space, the unique sound world of Howells must be retained, and full advantage should be taken of opportunities for an expansive and rich sound. The effect may be dreamy but the sound should never be vague. Tempos may be adjusted to accommodate more or less resonant spaces, although a sense of forward impetus should never be lost. The organ parts are similarly open to interpretation, having only the most general of guidelines from the composer. Where editorial interventions have been thought helpful they are indicated by the use of square brackets, particularly where a clearer indication of performance practice is useful. However, there is a great deal of room for interpretation in the Services, a process to which Howells was sympathetic.

Howells was a great admirer of the newly emerging choral sound being developed by David Willcocks and George Guest in Cambridge from the late 1940s onwards. This new style relied on a clean style of singing, avoiding the portamento ('scooping') that was then common. The notation reflects this desire for precision, particularly in relation to phrasing and dynamics. Performers should note how the last note of a phrase is often tied over to a quaver at the start of the following beat. This stylistic trait – which Howells shares with Vaughan Williams – may indicate the placing of the final consonant, just after the beat. Equally it may replicate the effect of a note dying away into the performance space rather than being abruptly cut off. The use of a momentary hum through a final consonant of an 'n' or an 'm' on such tied notes would aid a subtle, resonant effect. Although a wide range of dynamics is used, they should always be approached sensitively, with constant attention to the roundness of the tone and beauty of the phrasing.

Underlying the music is a sense of line and growth through each phrase, and this is at the heart of any effective interpretation. In polyphonic sections Howells' textures require each part of the choir to make a specific contribution, with an approach more like that of a collection of soloists than general groupings of singers. This feature suggests the influence of his extensive editing of Tudor church music. Where writing is homophonic, however, the line is led from the top, and this must be taken into account when considering the balance of the parts.

Magnificat and Nunc Dimittis

for St Paul's Cathedral

Magnificat

Herbert Howells
(1892–1983)

God _____ my _____ Sa - viour. For he _____ hath _ re -
God _____ my __ Sa - viour. For he _____ hath _ re -
God _____ my ___ Sa - viour. For he _____ hath _ re -
_____ my __ Sa - viour. For he _____ hath _ re -

- gard - ed the low - li - ness _____ of his hand - maid - en. _____
- gard - ed the low - li - ness _____ of his hand - maid - en. _____
- gard - ed the low - li - ness _____ of his hand - maid - en. _____
- gard - ed the low - li - ness _____ of his hand - maid - en. _____

Sw.

Man.

Gt. to Ped. off

(1) *poco rubato,* not accented

10

12

(1) Rhythm originally ○ in all voices. Amended editorially.

allargando

Nunc Dimittis

20

poco più mosso

Glo - - ry be_ to the Fa - ther

Glo - - ry be to the Fa - ther

Glo - - ry be_ to the Fa - ther

Glo - - ry be to the Fa - ther

poco più mosso

f marc.

and to_____ the Son,_____

and to_____ the Son,_____

and to_____ the Son,_____

and to_____ the Son,_____

poco

allargando

allargando

October 1951

Magnificat and Nunc Dimittis

for the Collegiate Church of Saint Peter in Westminster

Magnificat

Herbert Howells
(1892–1983)

a tempo, tranquillo

(1) reawakening

Nunc Dimittis

(1) reawakening

Composed specially for the Church Music Society Jubilee Festival Service at Westminster Abbey, 17 May 1956

Magnificat and Nunc Dimittis

set to music in the key of B minor

Magnificat

Herbert Howells
(1892–1983)

he hath scat - tered the proud___ in the i - ma - gi - na - tion of their

he hath scat - tered the proud in the i - ma - gi - na - tion of their

he hath scat - tered the proud___ in the i - ma - gi - na - tion of their

he hath scat - tered the proud in the i - ma - gi - na - tion of their

hearts.___ He hath___ put down___ the

hearts.___ He hath___ put down___ the

hearts.___ He hath___ put down___ the

hearts.___ He hath___ put down___ the

60

to our fore - fa - thers,___ A - bra-ham___ and his seed,___

dim. e rall.   Tempo I, risoluto

for___ ev - - er.___

Tempo I, risoluto

dim. e rall.

Nunc Dimittis

allargando

(XII. 1955)